London's Life

TWO FAMILIES STILL EQUALS ONE

BY SAMELLA STAFFORD

The contents of this work, including, but not limited to, the accuracy of events, people, and places depicted; opinions expressed; permission to use previously published materials included; and any advice given or actions advocated are solely the responsibility of the author, who assumes all liability for said work and indemnifies the publisher against any claims stemming from publication of the work.

All Rights Reserved

Copyright © 2022 by Samella Stafford

No part of this book may be reproduced or transmitted, downloaded, distributed, reverse engineered, or stored in or introduced into any information storage and retrieval system, in any form or by any means, including photocopying and recording, whether electronic or mechanical, now known or hereinafter invented without permission in writing from the publisher.

Dorrance Publishing Co
585 Alpha Drive
Pittsburgh, PA 15238
Visit our website at *www.dorrancebookstore.com*

ISBN: 978-1-6376-4104-0
eISBN: 978-1-6376-4945-9

London's Life

TWO FAMILIES STILL EQUALS ONE

My name is London. I have a mommy and a daddy. But we don't all live together.

When I was a baby my mommy and daddy "broke up", that's what Mommy told me.

So now I have two homes. I live with Mommy half the week and I live with Daddy the other half.

When I'm at Mommy's house, we have lots of fun together! We play dolls and read books and she always makes me my favorite breakfast: pancakes!

We run errands together and take trips to visit all our family. I love being with Mommy.

When I'm at Daddy's house, we have so much fun together too! He takes me and my big brother AJ to the trampoline park and lets me play video games with them.

We play wrestle and I practice how to throw a right hook. He tells me I'm his Princess and gives me lots of kisses! I love being with Daddy.

When Mommy and Daddy are around each other I really like it too. They throw me the best birthday parties together and both come watch me dance ballet.

We even all get to be together for some holidays and family events and that makes me very happy.

My big brother AJ has a different mommy than me but sometimes Mommy takes both of us to do fun things together too.

Sometimes I think about what it would be like if Mommy and Daddy were together all the time and I wouldn't have to go to two homes.

But then I think about how much I am loved and how happy I am, and I know everything is great just the way it is. I love my family!

Printed in the USA
CPSIA information can be obtained
at www.ICGtesting.com
LVHW071128080923
756304LV00027B/76